Beauty of
Iowa

Beauty of
Iowa

Text: Brian Berger
Concept & Design: Robert D. Shangle

Revised Edition
First Printing, October, 1991
Published by LTA Publishing Company
2735 S.E. Raymond Street; Portland, Oregon 97202
Robert D. Shangle, Publisher

"Learn about America in a beautiful way."

This book features the photography of
James Blank
Shangle Photographics

Library of Congress Cataloging-in-Publication Data
Berger, Brian
　　Beauty of Iowa / text, Brian Berger; concept & design, Robert D. Shangle.
　　Revised Edition of Beautiful Iowa.
　　　　p.　　cm.
　　ISBN 1-55988-027-9 (hardbound): $19.95. — ISBN 1-55988-026-0 (paperback):
$9.95
　　　1. Iowa — Description and travel — 1981 — Views. I. Shangle, Robert D. II. Title.
F622.B48　1991
917.7704'33 — dc20　　　　　　　　　　　　　　　　　　　91-24999
　　　　　　　　　　　　　　　　　　　　　　　　　　　　　CIP

Copyright © 1991 by LTA Publishing Company
Production, Concept and Distribution by LTA Publishing Company, Portland, Oregon.
Printed in Thailand. This book produced as the major component of the "World Peace and
Understanding" program of Beauty of America Printing Company, Portland, Oregon.

Contents

Introduction

"[Iowa is] something more than the world's *popcorn* center . . ." said Phil Strong, in his book *Hawkeyes*, and indeed it is. The state is home for a hardy, mostly conservative, sometimes obstinate, but thoroughly honest breed of Iowans that have sprung from the seeds of American and European ancestry.

Iowa's agricultural richness is due, in great part, to the efforts of a gathering of more than 20 nationalities that have reached into the state's black earth, America's "Heartland," to extract a yield that now accounts for a large portion of the nation's food supply. It is this same yield that has fattened Iowa's corn-fed hogs and created a cattle market second to that of Texas. Surprisingly though, more than 32 million acres of the state's "grade one" farmland is in crops. Iowa's industry claims more workers than does agriculture. Its industrial population upstages its agricultural output by many times. Once the town was home for only about five percent of Iowa's population. Now, over 50 percent have abandoned their rural beginnings for the cities, due to the growing industrial economy.

Iowa has a cultural side, although it is perhaps overshadowed by the state's agricultural origins. It is the birthplace or early home of some of the nation's best writers: Ruth Suckow, Thomas Beer, Emerson Hough, Ross Santee, Carl Van Vechten, and the list goes on. Some have vividly captured the picturesque sweep of Iowa's colorful landscape, using it as a framework for portrayals of its equally colorful citizens.

It is the land from which Iowa's culture has flowered, and which has become the magic lure for visitors to this heartland. Bounded on the east by the waters of the Mississippi and on the west by the waters of the Missouri, Iowa's rich, rolling, and colorful tablelands can be seen from the air, a patchwork quilt of freshly plowed or newly sprouting fields. Vistas of subtle greens, cut by the sinuous paths of small streams, contrast against geometrically designed plots of furrowed, dark browns. Autumn is colored with a bright, waving sea — millions of stalks of tall, hybrid corn, broken only by islands of red farm buildings. Where the Mississippi carves its winding path past the cities of Dubuque, Clinton, and Davenport, the trees take on the colors of the season, displaying brilliant mixes of gold, orange, rust, and subdued tangerine. To the west, lying in deep layers on the bluffs that overlook the Missouri River, the yellowish deposits of loess (glacial silt) glow.

Iowa's backroads will lead one through many of the state's farming communities, known to be fertile hunting grounds for the antique buff. Farm auctions sometimes disclose preserved examples of the furniture art, old clocks, and unique glassware items, some of which may have been transported with great care in the wagons of Iowa's first settlers. These same backroads will disclose garage sales and "flea markets," which will offer the visitor another rich source of the hidden treasures to be found in these rural areas.

But visitors will find Iowa's true richness to be its people. For those who take the time to accept their hospitality, they will find sincere warmth and friendliness.

Bred of the soil, nurtured in an atmosphere of decades of mutual help, Iowans seem totally removed from the social distinctions that have created distrust and formed the protective veneer that is common to more populous areas. They exude a mid-western easiness that speaks of a contentment built of trust, and a deep awareness of the special bounty of the soil on which they live.

Brian Berger

The Landscape

To view Iowa's flat, cultivated, and crop-yielding vistas today, one would never suspect that, at an earlier time, this same soil nourished great forests. Black-ash, elm, and cottonwood fringed the borders of its rivers, while hickory and oak covered large areas of uplands. As far as the eye could reach, the tall grasses of the prairie lands stood. Breast high, the thick stalks could swallow a man in their billowing extravagance. Bison moved upon the landscape like a great, undulating brown carpet. Magnificent herds of elk grazed on the lushness of the shrubs and grasses. Large gatherings of water birds found a peaceful resting place in the sparkling lakes during their long migrations, their coming and going monitored by meadow-jumping mice and pocket gophers, living among the tall grasses bordering these waters. Early Iowa settlers hailed the sight of this new land with awed exuberance, and called it "the newest, strangest, most delightful, sternest, most wonderful thing in the world. . . ." It has been read that others described it with a more sobering appraisal: "I do not know anything that struck me more forcibly than the sensation of solitude. . . . I was perfectly alone, and could see nothing in any direction but sky and grass."

The forests have now disappeared, and the tall grasses have been replaced by a patchwork of colorful fields, yet Iowa is still a land of extraordinary beauty. The state's empty horizons and flat lands are the perfect platforms for viewing the drama of the seasons played across a limitless expanse of sky.

It is known that four massive glacial intrusions (the last only about 25,000 years ago) were responsible for the rich mix of Iowa's soils, sands, silts, and clay. Under the pressure of millions of tons of ice, moving at less than a snail's pace for thousands of years, the rocks and soils beneath were mixed and pulverized, and in the process, transported thousands of miles from their original sources. As the massive slabs of ice moved south, they encountered continually warmer weather, until, after covering most of the region that now includes Iowa, they began retreating and melting. During this melting process, the great deposits of sand and gravel, as well as gigantic boulders that had been pushed before this natural earth-moving machine, formed the "drift," which became the foundation for the state's rich soil. During the long, interglacial periods, weathering and oxidation further refined these deposits, spreading them evenly over the landscape. The last of these massive deposits of drift (known as the Iowan and Mankato) contained the usual mix of rock and sand, but did not undergo the weathering process of the previous deposits, forming instead a rich black soil, composed partly by alluvial deposits (laid down when vast inland seas once covered the area) and decayed vegetable matter.

The ground needed only the proper mix of climatic conditions to bring forth the land's eventual abundance of plant life. Those conditions were met with Iowa's warm and moist months of spring and summer (71 percent of Iowa's annual precipitation falls from April through September), and a water table that stayed near the surface, owing to the flatness of the land. Great storms appeared as towering walls of black clouds on the horizon, the air crackled with their energies, and in their aftermath of airborn violence, the nourishing rains fell in wind-whipped torrents, deeply saturating the soil. The winters brought biting cold temperatures, at times plunging to $-43°$ Fahrenheit, while in the summers, the land would shimmer in temperatures near $113°$ Fahrenheit. But these were extremes, and the mean temperature was 50°. The land retained the heat of its summers, and this contributed greatly to the length of Iowa's growing season.

The tall grasses began to sprout: bluestem, switch grass, Indian grass, some reaching to heights of 14 feet. Near the borders of lakes and rivers, willow, honey-locust, coffee trees, black-ash, and elms grew in shady abundance. Higher ground, in addition to the thick forests of oak and hickory, supported white and green ash, butternut, ironwood, and hackberry. In time, familiar animal life appeared on the scene, some to inhabit Iowa to the present day, others to eventually find extinction at the hands of man. Feeding on the great herds of buffalo, pronghorn, and elk were the gray, and now extinct, white wolf. In the forested areas, grizzly bears held supreme reign over their lush feeding grounds. A beautiful symbiosis of plant and animal life had thus evolved, awaiting only the white man's empire-building efforts to upset its delicate balance.

Some History

As early as 1673, part of Iowa's northeastern border had been explored by the French-Canadian trapper Louis Joliet, and a party of six other men headed by Pere Jacques Marquette. Then, in 1680, the French explorer La Salle, in following the length of the Mississippi to its mouth, explored the shoreline that was later to become the eastern border of Iowa. More than a century passed before Meriwether Lewis and his associate William Clark explored Iowa's western border on their expedition up the Missouri River. It would be their job to compile a detailed report for President Thomas Jefferson concerning the land so recently acquired (1803) from the French, and known as the Louisiana Purchase. The Indians of the region, having been pushed from their lands to the east by the rapid influx of colonists, would soon feel the full weight of their frenzied expansionist policy. Pursuing a dream of riches, and heeding tales of fertile lands for the taking, a trickle at first, and then a flood of immigrants poured through the Cumberland Gap of the Appalachian Mountains. This marked the beginnings of the westward movement and that of an empire for the white man.

Not all white men who ventured into the region of Iowa disturbed its environment; the early trappers, hunters and traders, although taking their toll of wildlife, lived very much the same life as the Indians — one of harmony with the wilderness. Many inter-married with the Indians, while doing business with the American Fur Company's trading posts, a number of which eventually developed into cities: Council Bluffs, Sioux

City, Eddyville, Muscatine, and Keokuk among them. The Des Moines River region was especially rich in fur-bearing animals, and quickly became Iowa's fur-trading center.

By 1821 Iowa still had no identity of its own; it was part of the Territory of Missouri established in 1812. Legally still Indian land, the vast prairies of Iowa had not experienced any great intrusion by the white man. But by 1833 the immigrants, after gaining access to part of eastern Iowa through a treaty known as the Black Hawk Purchase, commenced settling the land in large numbers. By 1840 nearly 43,000 settlers had laid out claims, and Iowans had successfully lobbied to create their own territory. Two years later, the settlers had pushed their way west some 90 miles into the Iowa wilderness and were hard at work breaking the tough prairie sod, a task that sometimes needed seven yoke of oxen to be accomplished. The idea of statehood was finding rapid favor among settlers, and by May of 1846, boundaries had been drawn up and approved by Congress. Iowa was admitted into the Union on August 3, 1846.

Towns began to rise around grist mills, and prospectors enriched the economy by bringing the wealth of their gold diggings into the state. The soil, so laboriously carried to the area by the advance of great glaciers, during a period of thousands of years, was now producing a golden harvest that grew taller than any other place in the world. Bolstered by the many Europeans looking to escape the oppression of their homelands, the population by 1850 was nearing the 200,000 mark. Caught in the tide of settlers that were sweeping toward the Pacific Ocean to claim their "Manifest Destiny," the Indians and the buffalo were being pushed farther westward. During the 1850s the heaviest wave of settlers flowed into the northern portion of the state, establishing Czech, French, Danish, and German communities. Schools were built, businesses erected, and a spirit

14

of mutual cooperation was showing itself in community functions. It was a spirit that is so much a part of Iowa townships today.

During this same period, the railroads were racing to complete the transcontinental route. Towns followed in the path of their tracks, and by May of 1869, the Union Pacific and the Central Pacific railways had joined their rails at Promontory Summit, Utah. It would bring settlers west by the thousands. While the Union and Central Pacific railroads were busy with their continent-spanning race, other tracks were being laid by the Illinois Central and Rock Island railroads, making Des Moines, Cedar Rapids, Fort Dodge, and Waterloo into busy railroad centers. Iowa's population had grown an additional million from its 1850 figure, and coal mining, together with construction of numerous factories, were adding substantially to the moneys of its farm produce. The late 1870s saw the railroads creating stiff competition for products once handled entirely by river traffic. To eliminate possible overcharging practices by these essential movers of goods, "Granger laws" were passed, setting rate limits on shipments.

By the 1900s Iowa was experiencing the greatest growth of any previous period. Its industries were expanding, well-built roads were speeding up automobile transportation, and its primary crops — corn, wheat, hay, potatoes, barley, and oats — were bringing top market prices. The mood of the people was one of optimism; a "New Era" of unprecedented wealth was exhibiting itself in Iowa's growing economy. Jobs were plentiful, and the belief was held that everyone could be rich. But then something unforeseen happened. Beginning around 1920, farm prices began to drop as industrial prosperity continued its upward surge. The farmer, caught in the position of falling income and increased prices for labor and goods, was slowly being squeezed between "a rock and a hard place." Many, unable to meet their mortgage payments, experienced foreclosure. They became renters on farms that they had given their best years to build.

What the Iowa farmers were experiencing in the early '20s, the country was soon to feel during the great depression. Almost 13 percent of Iowa farms were auctioned off, while more than 25 percent underwent foreclosure. To compound matters, 1934 and 1936 were drought years, and the already beleaguered farmer was pulled still deeper into the economic quagmire. At its worst, the depression caused almost half of Iowa's farmland to become tenant operated. Finally, the federal government, realizing a need to prevent the absolute economic ruin of the farmer, provided Federal subsidies that pumped new life into the farm belt.

The crisis had passed, but the years between 1938 and 1945 would remain a time of economic uncertainty for the farmer. Helping to ease the doubts of the future was the Iowan camaraderie, which had lightened up the burden of the depression years. The country store was a place for farmers to gather after the long hours in the fields, where stories could be swapped. The store itself was a conversation piece, with a seemingly endless collection of interesting, if not essential, items. Saturday nights might find a great gathering of neighbors sharing conversation over an array of dinner fare, such as Graham Hutton details in his book, *Midwest at Noon*: ". . . fresh mushroom soup; two kinds of chicken or pork; lima and string beans, baked potatoes, corn biscuits, preserve of baby strawberries and butter with the biscuits; salad of lettuce with fresh cranberry and pomegranate jello thereon; ice cream and maple syrup, or three kinds of pie. . . ."

These would be remembered as the good years, the feelings that have persisted in the homespun friendliness of Iowa's people. Their

16

Famous Old Amana Home Museum

Iowa Farm Country

Botanical Center, Des Moines

Famous Old Fort, Fort Dodge

At Pella

In An Iowa Amish Community

Rose Garden at the Art Center, Des Moines

Sabula, On The Mississippi River

Des Moines Skyline

State Capitol Building, Des Moines

Storm Lake

County Courthouse, Dubuque

Sailing on Grey's Lake

Cedar Rapids

Vander Veer Park, Davenport

The Old State Capitol Building, Iowa City

Spirit Lake

Herbert Hoover Birthplace, West Branch

Famous "Little Brown Church in the Vale," Nashua

Bellevue, on the Mississippi River

Mississippi River at Burlington

Ottumwa

Graceland College, Lamoni

Lidke Grist Mill, North of Decorah

Lake Okoboji

Pella

University of Northern Iowa, Cedar Falls

Governor's Mansion, Des Moines

John Wayne's Home, Winterset

Locks on the Mississippi River at Keokuk

Salisbury House, Des Moines

Mason City

Kalona Historical Village

View of Mississippi River from Eagle Point Park, Dubuque

Drake University, Des Moines

Iowa State University, Ames

McGregor, on the Mississippi

Herbert Hoover Presidential Library, West Branch

Missouri River, North of Council Bluffs

Near Mount Vernon

Historic "Goldenrod," Birthplace of 4H, Clarinda

Farming near Pella

Wild Cat Den State Park

Northeast Iowa Farmland

Grist Mill at Wild Cat Den State Park, Muscatine

Fort Atkinson

Farming near Maquoketa

Bellevue

strong religious convictions, hospitality, trust, belief in hard work and equally hard play, have filled Iowa with their optimism, and reaped from its black earth the harvest of the good life.

Towns Arise

The earliest examples of Iowa architecture were the rough-hewn log or sod houses of the pioneers. Where the prairie was an uninterrupted sea of tall grasses, especially in the northern and western portions of the state, sod was the chosen building material. The tightly packed earth was excellent for cutting into block-like sections, which, when piled, formed the walls of the dwelling. Poles were then erected to form the roof structure, then overlaid with thinner sections of sod. The material, though it created a rather dark and moist interior, was a perfect insulator, keeping the interior cool in summer and warm in winter. Occasionally, glass windows were installed to lighten the interior, the first signs of affluence in this newly settled territory.

Where trees were plentiful, roughly cut logs were the choice of the home builder; piled to a convenient height, the gaps were then filled with splinters of wood mixed with clay and straw. The roof was overlaid with split wood to form shingles, and a chimney was erected with available stones. Gradually, lumber cut to even thickness supplemented the heavily timbered cabins, and brick and stone came into common usage. Towns would spring from these early beginnings, drawing many from the farms to the taskmaster of an expanding industrialism. The vast areas of prairie grasses were soon plowed under, burned, or overgrazed. Forests were felled to provide the lumber needed for building towns, which were fast mushrooming from Iowa's rich soil. The cities suddenly grew with the influx of immigrants seeking opportunities denied them in their homelands.

All a man needed to be was resourceful and hardworking in order to find that social questions, restrictions, or conventions were limiting factors that need not concern him. Many who first settled the immense Iowa prairies would live to see the internal combustion engine revolutionize transportation, farming and industry; and with it, the increased riches of an industrial economy.

Des Moines, the capital of Iowa, and Polk County seat, saw its early beginnings as Fort Des Moines, erected in May of 1843. A gathering point for immigrant trains headed for California, it was also a way station for those who sought to strike it rich in the gold fields. The city officially became the state capital in January of 1858, and owed its early growth to the Des Moines River running through it, making the city an important cargo center for the steamboats that used this waterway. An important agricultural center early on, today state government is Des Moines' chief business. Referred to at times as the "Hartford of the West," the city also is important for its printing, banking, and insurance companies. Visitors will find the Iowa of the past and that of the future reposing side by side. Located on Rural Route 1, the Living History Farms reflect the Iowa of the settler in the 1840s Pioneer Farm, that of the early 20th century in the 1900 Farm, and the technology of the future in the farm of Today and Tomorrow. At the Des Moines Center of Science and Industry, children and adults will find fascinating displays of astronomy, physics, and computer science, many of which are designed for "hands on" participation.

Besides the architectural uniqueness of Des Moines' capital building, one will find the height of Victorian lavishness in the city's Terrace Hill Mansion (now the official Governor's residence), open on most weekdays to the public. In addition there is the Civic Center, a major art center, and the Iowa Historical Building, with artifacts and memorabilia of the state's pioneer past.

Centrally located in the northeastern sector of the state, the Waterloo-Cedar Falls community was originally begun by George W. Hanna, who built a homesite in 1845 on the west bank of the Cedar River. Other settlers joined the Hanna family, and the community was given the name Prairie Rapids. Sometime later, while petitioning for a post office, the name Waterloo was thought to have a better ring to it, and was so designated. The area is a modern industrialized center today, but has not sacrificed any of its livability. Recreational opportunities in the area are abundant. There are over 2,600 acres of parkland within the cities where one can fish and boat on the beautiful Cedar River. From the area's modest beginnings as a center for sawmills and flour mills, the Waterloo-Cedar Falls community has grown into one of Iowa's chief industrial centers, employing 30 percent of the area's work force. The community's largest industry is the John Deere Waterloo Tractor Works (the largest wheel tractor plant in the world).

Early on, the Cedar Rapids-Marion area, spreading east and west from the banks of the Cedar River, drew power from the waterway to run its grist and sawmills. Less than 17 years after the first survey of the city, the railroad reached its doorstep. The railroad would bring a lessening of river traffic and an expanding interest in manufacturing and marketing. Agriculture still plays a substantial role in the economy of these two cities today, but their almost depression-proof economy is also strengthened by over 200 industries contributing to the millions of dollars worth of goods that are exported from the Cedar Rapids area yearly.

As bustling manufacturing centers, these cities also offer a wealth of interesting leisure activities. Boating, camping, and fishing at the Coralville Dam and Reservoir, just south of Cedar Rapids, will reward one with glimpses of an abundant population of whitetail deer, waterfowl, and other colorful species of aquatic wildlife. Fishermen will find the area to be plentiful in bass, bluegill, crappie, and channel catfish; while the upper portions of the reservoir's 4,100 acres are devoted to the beauties of the Hawkeye Wildlife Area, a refuge for migratory waterfowl. Additionally, 62 other parks covering more than 3,200 acres, offer a wide range of activities, including swimming, golfing, tennis, and the chance to enjoy their scenic pathways. Unhurried, beautiful, and clean, Cedar Rapids and Marion are cities where the American spirit of "can do" thrives.

Having a beginning as a fur-trading center run by the American Fur Company, Davenport (now a dual municipality with the city of Bettendorf, adjacent to it) was officially founded in 1836. The first of Iowa's cities to be serviced by the railroad, after a bridge was built to span the Mississippi from Illinois, it rapidly grew into a commercial and industrial center. With the cities of Rock Island and Moline, Illinois just across the river from Davenport/Bettendorf, the area is popularly known as the "Quad-Cities" group. Davenport is primarily a trading and shopping center today, but retains much of its early flavor with numerous examples of historic architecture that grace the city's clean streets. For those wishing to experience some of the drama of the Mark Twain era, a river excursion aboard a sternwheeler will remind one of the colorful past of the Mississippi River gamblers, while one enjoys the scenery of the river's tree-lined shores.

Another river town, but this one at the junction of the Big Sioux and Floyd rivers, where they join the waters of the "Big Muddy" (Missouri River), is the important livestock and grain center, Sioux City. During the 1860s Sioux City became a supply base for travelers journeying overland, or arriving by steamboat, after negotiating the Missouri's tricky waters. Pilots who knew this river could sometimes earn as much as $1,200 a month for their skills, far surpassing even a captain's salary of $200. The Pacific Railroad reached the city in 1868, and two years later was joined by the tracks of the Illinois Central, making the area an important shipping point. Billed as the "cultural and recreational mecca of the Great Plains," the city offers visitors acres of parklands, interesting historic sites, river excursions, and a chance to shop many interesting stores that serve a 50-county area.

Following the Missouri River south, one will encounter the busy manufacturing city of Council Bluffs. Developed on the site of an early trading post, the city owes its early growth as a town to a Mormon population that grew to nearly 8,000 by 1852, before they abandoned it to join Brigham Young in Utah.

Since World War II there has been a steady influx of young people who have abandoned their farm upbringing to find jobs within the diversified industries that have grown rapidly in and around Iowa's larger cities. Due to important technological advances in farming practices, fewer hands are needed to produce 50 percent more crops than were needed two decades ago. During the same period, industrial production has undergone a three-fold increase.

One will find that even the small cities have attracted some of the top 500 manufacturers: Clinton with Du Pont, Allied Structural Steel, and Hawkeye Chemical Company; Fort Madison with Schaeffer Pen; and Newton with Maytag washers. Others are fast dropping their small town image: Fort Dodge with its diversified shopping areas; Ames with its new factories, retail stores, and the influx of students to its Iowa State University. Still others offer unique exhibits of historical interest: Spillville with its display of hand-carved Bily Clocks; The Amana Colonies with its old world flavor and many interesting gift shops; Mt. Pleasant with its Heritage Museum housing one of the nation's largest collections of steam traction engines; and the Grotto of Redemption, at West Bend, sometimes referred to as "the Eighth Wonder of the World." Iowa's cities have grown rapidly, and are still growing rapidly; yet most have retained the main ingredients that mark them as communities with livability — their small-town characteristics.

Simple Pleasures

Iowa's Indians called this region of changing colors, climatic extremes, and unlimited vistas "The Beautiful Land." Changed as it is from an era of tall grasses sweeping to unbroken horizons, and without the forests that fell to the axes of the first great rush of settlers, Iowa now greets the visitor with a landscape of different beauty. Multi-hued fields of colorful crops change imperceptibly as the waning daylight adds subtle shadings to their ripening forms. Along the banks of the Mississippi River, a declining sun darkens distant trees to silhouettes, igniting a golden pathway across the waters, and a rich golden haze casts its warmth upon the land. When autumn touches this land with its gradually deepening chill, the orange-red and yellow leaves begin to brighten roadways and outline the course of the state's rivers. The sky takes on a blueness that pains the eye. Light winds play tunes against the dry, dying leaves. Stoked to an orange glow, fireplaces tinge the air with a mild, smoky fragrance. It is a comfortable time; a time of nature's simple joy, and one the visitor to Iowa may find the most inviting.

A popular route for the tourist any time of the year, U.S. Highway 30 cuts a colorful east-west path across the middle of the state. On Iowa's western border, near the junction of Highway 75 and Highway 30, spreads the 7,800-acre Desota National Wildlife Refuge. This refuge, providing a temporary home for a migrating population of nearly 400,000 geese and one million ducks annually, will reward visitors with glimpses of some of Iowa's native wildlife species, such as beaver, raccoon, deer, or the elusive fox. Here are the remains of the steamboat *Bertrand*, which laid for nearly 100 years beneath the Missouri's muddy waters, until it was discovered in 1968. Many of the nearly two million artifacts, which have been salvaged from its hull, are on display for the visitor.

Farther east, the town of Jefferson is the location of the Mahaney Memorial Carillon Tower. An unique architectural work, it serves as an observation platform from which to view the colors of the surrounding countryside. Travelers will also want to visit the displays in the town's telephone museum and delight in the fragrance and color of its rose garden. Just down the road, near the town of Boone, Ledges State Park offers room to stretch one's legs while studying unusual rock formations and enjoying the wooded surroundings. Located on the east edge of the park, the Iowa Wildlife Research Station offers interesting exhibits of some of the state's native animals, fowl, and reptiles.

Just southeast of Cedar Rapids, Lake McBride State Park (part of the network of the Coralville Reservoir) is a popular swimming, boating, fishing, and camping spot. Nearby, Palisades-Kepler State Park provides the visitor with hiking trails that take one past colorful limestone bluffs, Indian burial mounds, the remains of an ancient coral reef, and numerous caves. During the winter months, the park becomes an attraction for skiers, the snow settling into its deep timbered valleys. Close by, Mt. Vernon is the starting point for motorists wishing to follow the Iowa Heritage Trail, a routed auto trip that will take you past some of Iowa's cultural, industrial, educational, and religious heritage. Between Mt. Vernon and the city of Clinton, on the Mississippi River, more than a dozen other county parks and recreation areas dot the countryside, many with facilities for the camper.

Travelers to northwestern Iowa will find it a land of many lakes. Gouged from the land by the advance of great glaciers, many of them resemble low bowls filled with water, surrounded by thick forest growth. The largest of these bodies of water, Spirit Lake, is a glistening 5,700-acre pool. Popular as a center for watersports, the lake is historically interesting as the site of the infamous Spirit Lake Massacre, in which 42 settlers lost their lives to a band of renegade Sioux Indians. Known as Siouxland on state recreational guides, the area is popular for its winter sport activities, and the quaint, small-town festivals throughout the region, celebrating everything from Irishmen to tulips.

Lined by high bluffs with their forested greenery, and dotted with small islands, each with their own miniature forests, the Mississippi River winds its border-lining way the length of Iowa's western edge. Flowing past an area of industrial towns amid a patchwork of farms nestled into rolling hills, the Mississippi served as Iowa's highway of commerce in its early days, until replaced by the rapid growth of the railroads. Beginning as a 20-foot-wide trickle in the lake country of Minnesota, it courses some 2,350 miles to where its silt-laden waters empty into the Gulf of Mexico. The river is still endowed with the heritage of its early riverboat days, and visitors along her banks and backroads will find that she's alive with festivals, celebrations, and homespun hospitality. Towboats and barges have now replaced the more romantic sternwheelers, and one can spend a quiet afternoon watching their traffic move millions of tons of petroleum, coal, salt, molasses, asphalt, steel, and ammonia upstream. Those moving downstream carry huge quantities of grain.

Many of the small towns that line the Mississippi's winding course have names that recall the romance of its pioneer era: Harpers Ferry, once a community of pearl fishermen; Waukon Junction, a railroad stop a mile from where Indian pictographs were discovered at Paint Rock; Guttenberg, named for the famous German printer; Bellevue, formally Bell View, where in the late 1830s a gang of rustlers and a posse of vigilantes fought it out after a series of horse nabbings; Le Claire, the early home of Buffalo Bill (William F. Cody); Buffalo, known for its pearl-button industry; Fairport, one time known as "Jug Town" for its pottery works started by John Feustel, a German immigrant; and Montrose, one of the earliest white settlements in the state.

For the visitor who would travel to Iowa in every season, many annual events in the state's smaller towns will brighten their visit. During the months of January and February, the towns of Cresco and Esterville host their Snow Festivals, where snowmobile, skiing, and ice-skating competitions are topped off by sparkling examples of ice sculpture artistry. March finds the population of Emmetsburg dressed in green, while marching in the St. Patrick's Day Grand Parade, and judging entrants in the Miss St. Patrick's Day Pageant. May is Tulip Festival time at the towns of Pella and Orange City; dressed in Dutch costume, their residents parade to the music of a street organ, accompanying it with the clomping sounds of hundreds of wooden shoes. Tulips by the thousands brighten community tulip beds, and the atmosphere recalls the strong Dutch heritage of these people.

Summer in Iowa is a time for revelry on the grand scale. Billed as the home of the "World's Largest Street Fair," the town of Keokuk, in June, displays a choice array of arts and crafts, agricultual products, and the beauties of its horticultural yield. A Scandinavian smorgasbord, parade, model airplane show, and the state's largest hobby craft exhibit are a few of the goings-on during Eagle Grove's Scandinavian Dager Celebration. Keosauqua is host for the Van Buren County Summer Arts Festival. The city extends an invitation to the nation during this time. Tours are conducted to the many artists' galleries throughout the country, allowing visitors to see firsthand many of the area's painters, sculptors, potters, weavers, and carvers at work. In addition, there is a Sunday morning fly-in for those interested in participating in its air show, or in displaying antique and homebuilt aircraft. July is the time for the Nordic Fest days at Decorah, when the Norwegian heritage of this community is displayed in the wearing of colorful costumes, Norwegian delicacies served smorgasbord-style, and the excitement of fast-paced folk dances.

August brings the National Hot Air Balloon Championships to Indianola, now the permanent home for this colorful display of brightly hued balloons. The visitor will see balloonists test their knowledge of wind currents and their skills at maneuvering in a race, which is awesome to behold. If Mulligan Stew is ambrosia to your taste buds, then the National Hobo Convention at Britt welcomes you with more than 500 gallons of it (served free to the public) and a chance to watch the King and Queen of Hobodom be selected to head a grand parade that draws hobos from all parts of the country. The Iowa Championship Rodeo is also in the month of August. Held at the town of Sidney, it brings the nation's top cowboys to its outdoor arena to test their roping and riding skills. Knoxville means fast cars and big money purses during the four days of the city's National Spring Car Championships. Enticing some of the best sprint-car drivers in the nation, they run qualifying trials for three days, until summoned to "put it on the line" in a dust raising, Saturday night final confrontation for the championship.

Autumn brings with it the Fort Madison, Tri-State Rodeo (Iowa, Missouri, and Illinois) and the pageantry of one of the state's largest parades, together with name entertainment during each performance.

The Amana Colonies hold their Oktoberfest during this time, with huge quantities of beer, wine, and flavorful German dishes to fuel the dancers and merry makers. At the end of September, Fort Atkinson hosts its "Rendezvous" — displaying period crafts and exhibits of the lifestyles of Iowa's early hunter-trappers. Things are kept lively with various types of frontier competition conducted throughout the two days of festivities.

William Carter, in *Middle West Country*, said of the midwest: "[It] is more than a physical area. It is a region of the heart. A home place: sometimes narrowly disapproving, but nurturing and loving, and preserving the style of the era before America moved away to the city." For the visitor to Iowa, it is a style that manifests itself as a combination of its land, its people, their forms of recreation and the towns they live in, that gives one this feeling of "a home place."

Iowa

State Capital: *Des Moines*
State Flower: *Wild Rose*
State Nickname: *Hawkeye State*
State Bird: *Eastern Goldfinch*

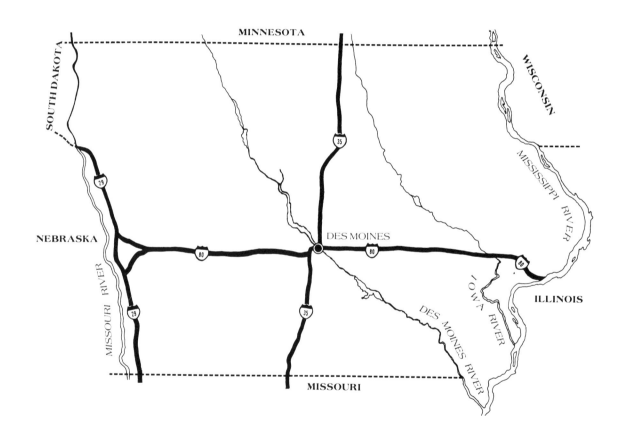